Conversations
with an Angel

By Cliff Woffenden

Typesetting and graphics by the author.

Published by Howling Moon Productions
Box 223
Nakusp, B.C.
V0G 1R0

Canadian Cataloging in Publication Data
Woffenden, Cliff, 1946-
Conversations with an Angel
ISBN: 978-0-9694585-7-9

1.   History 2. Autobiographical 3. My Life
1. Title.

ISBN: 978-0-9694585-7-9

Other books by Cliff Woffenden

But Now I See – a novel of alternative realities and shamanism

The Freedom of Responsibility – Spirituality and philosophy

A Pilgrim's Way - The Collected Works of

Ghost Peoples: The Sinixt, recovering from extinction – History of the local indigenous peoples of the Arrow Lakes and Slocan Valleys.

Crazier Than a Shithouse Rat – the Misadventures of a Bush Hippie

Index

Acknowledgments

I would like to thank all those who, by intent or by accident, help me understand what life is all about, what is real and what is truth. It has been a trip, to say the least. My teachers have been many and diverse. My lessons have been humbling and enlightening. Thank you one and all.

Introduction

This story basically wrote itself. I would get up in the morning excited to find out what was going to happen next. Cynthia represented all I had learned through books, teachers and experiences in life.

Conversation with an Angel

Pop Goes The Weasel

Another mind numbing day at the office and Rob was ready to vegetate in front of the idiot box for one more mind numbing evening. Rob's life was becoming so routinely dull that he resigned himself to the oblivion of his mind. He sat down in his orthopedically incorrect armchair, with his traditional bottle of beer, to watch the evening news.

As the anchor droned on and on about one tragedy after another, Rob's mind began to unravel. Something was terribly wrong with this picture. A series of unrelated images flashed inside his mind's eye. Alternating between the scenes of disaster and carnage on the tube, were images of children playing and flowers blooming, high mountain alpine meadows and suckling fawn, sun filled beaches and tropical rain forests. These images were so startlingly real and intense that they overpowered the TV screen. The images were bouncing back and forth at a rapidly increasing rate, causing a strobe effect in his head. He became overwhelmed by a sensation of nausea. Nothing made any sense.

Everything he thought he knew about life was caught in his throat. He felt like he had been suddenly transported to a totally alien reality and he had no points of reference by which to comprehend where he was or who he was. He looked helplessly about the room that had been so familiar a minute ago and he could not recognize a single thing in the context of his present state of mind.

He heard his voice say "This must be some really bad beer!" but it sounded like gobbley goop. He looked back at the TV and the announcer's face began to take on the appearance of a single celled amoeba, his mouth devouring the pixels on the screen like Pac Man on amphetamines.

Suddenly Rob had an epiphany - his mental enema to end all mental enemas. It all became perfectly and painfully clear. It was not his mind that was unraveling but the very fabric of reality as he understood it. The whole thing - Life as he thought he knew it - was a hoax of global proportions. His best friend, Barry, had said it many times before he died of an overdose of cocaine: "Life is but a joke and the joke is on you." Rob never could understand what he was talking about - until now.

"Holy shit!" he yelled at the TV. "I've been rotting my brain with this meaningless, brain eating drivel all of my life." Then a high pitch shriek rose up from the bowels of his being. Slowly and methodically it gained in pitch and volume until the TV tube imploded along with his mind.

When the smoke, thick with the acrid, nose hair singeing stench of burning plastic, cleared, he found himself standing in space. (How one stands in space is still a matter of conjecture but, nonetheless, Rob found himself in this awkward and intellectually perplexing situation.) Ahead were stars and planets, twinkling and winking like a billion little eyes, curious to know what this strange creature was doing invading their territory. Behind him he could feel the sun beating against the back of his skull. He looked around to his right. About a thousand miles away, was a round object he recognized as Earth.

8

It didn't even startle him. In fact he began to laugh; one of those deep belly laughs one gets when the great cosmic joke is realized. His laugh would have caused the entire population of the planet to join in, it was so real, so honest and so infectious but nobody noticed. They didn't even realize he was no longer among them.

What surprised him - only so slightly, mind you - was it didn't matter. He surveyed his new surroundings and felt whole and complete for the first time he could remember. There was no need to look to others for verification or approval. Rob knew he was not insane but even if he were, he preferred this new perspective to the old.

In some strange way he felt his life long suspicion, that there must be more to life than the mundane existence of jobs, taxes and bad relationships, was now being validated by the Universe itself. As he looked over at the bright, blazing Sun, he had the impression he was looking into the eye of God. A sense of peace and safety engulfed him. Then the eye winked at him!

****

He began to suspect he was not the first to find himself in this type of situation. He didn't think he was so special that the Universe had singled him out of all the other mortals on this planet. Others must have come before him. He was wondering why he had never heard of such experiences before when he felt a tap on his shoulder. He turned to see a beautiful and strangely familiar, young woman standing next to him.

Her voice was as soft as a flower petal against his ear, though her lips did not move. "Lovely, isn't it?"

The implication of her words flowed through him with the intensity of a nuclear blast. His head began to fill with every word ever spoken. He felt his head expand to accommodate the volume of it. He understood the meaning of every word. Then his head shrank as the meanings became so crystal clear and simple that all he could do was smile peacefully and release a long slow sigh.

His sense of identity ceased to exist along with his physical form. Rob became a meaningless concept. He was only aware of a growing sensation he was every person who ever lived. He comprehended everything with razor sharp clarity and with this clarity he realized he knew nothing at all.

He began to expand until his being encompassed the entire Universe. He became the Universe. He marveled at the immensity and beauty, the order and the chaos, of it all. Then he began to shrink until he became a grain of sand. The sand melted into glass from the intensity of the heat caused by his sudden compression. A rat crawled over the glass and he became the rat. He crawled up onto a pile of garbage and grew wings. He flew up into the sky, beyond his capacity to breath. He fell back toward the Earth, unceremoniously plunged into the ocean and swallowed by a fish with fluorescent eyes.

He experienced what it was like to be all things. He went through the food chain from microbe to Blue Whale, from nitrogen molecule to carrot, from mushroom mycelium to giant red wood. In a state of mind beyond thought, he felt the meaning of life. Simultaneously, he saw what a pointless frenzy of activity most people's lives, especially his own, had become.

Then he saw his TV implode with a flash and a fizzle... "Whomp!"

He looked about the room disappointed. 'This sucks,' he thought to himself. 'I would much rather be among the stars than in this rat hole.' It didn't look the same anymore. It was somehow unreal and he was uncomfortable. It no longer felt like home but a prison where he had wasted far too much of his time avoiding life. This realization caused him to decide then and there to make some radical changes.

He knew he could no longer live his life as he had. The TV's demise was such a clear metaphor. His entire existence, up until this moment, had been not only a lie but also a slow living death. To continue down this path of apathy could only end in rigor mortise.

He read, once, that ninety percent of all deaths could be attributed to suicide. Our bodies die due to the loss of a sense of wonder and enthusiasm for life. People who find no pleasure, who lack curiosity about life, give up and subconsciously attract accidents, illness and violence into their lives. Most people died long before their allotment of time had run out. He vowed not to make the same mistake, even if it killed him.

'Just kidding!' he sheepishly whispered to the sky.

In his heightened state of awareness, he knew, beyond a shadow of a doubt, that life was eternal and that death is a belief - a part of the lie. It was an absurd notion to him now. The only point in time we live and exist is right now, right here. Everything else is a fiction.

His mind began to reel with the possibilities opening up to him. Although he was not sure what they might be, exactly, he was sure that the narrow view of possibilities, within which he had been indoctrinated, was now blown to hell. Outside the straight jacket of conventional thought, lay a universe of ideas and experiences to explore.

He had no regrets for his past life. He had not known any better. But, with what he had just been through, if he did not act on the impulse to radically change the way he lived his life, he would die for sure.

He didn't fear death. He understood death was an intrinsic part of life - a doorway into greater possibilities. But if we waste our opportunity to gain wisdom and joy in this life, we are doomed to remain ignorant, even after death. As one philosopher once put it, if you are as dense as a brick in life, you will be as dense as a brick in death and will have to return to physical reality, lifetime after lifetime, until you get it. (What 'it' is, is what Rob intended to find out).

No, Rob had been given a second chance to experience Life and he was not going to waste another second of it. He was bound and determined to reach beyond his own limiting thoughts and beliefs, beyond the veil of lies imprisoning humanity and explore the brave new frontier (at least to him) waiting patiently on the other side.

He had no game plan. Nor did he fully understand what had just happen to him. He only knew he had to climb over the edge of his prison walls, beyond the confines of his own, self-imposed, restrictive beliefs. 'When confronted with a mountain, become a mountain climber!' he thought.

He decided he would dedicate his life to discovering just how far he could go, how much he could accomplish, just how vast this uncharted territory was. It was time for his journey of self-discovery to begin. He saw before him a road map to adventure written in disappearing ink. He knew the cosmic joke and, although he could not tell you what it was, it motivated every decision he made from that moment on.

****

All preparations were made. All loose ends were tied. He quit his job, terminated his lease and prepared his car for the open road. He was looking forward to the drive out west and to letting his life unfold as it would. He had no idea where he was going and he was very comfortable with that.

There was only one small thing left to do. He had, long ago, forgotten of its presence. It had been hiding behind the plants on the windowsill. With the plants safely secured to good homes, it was once again exposed to scrutiny. For almost ten years it sat, forgotten and abandoned. As he stood there staring at its delicate form, a rush of memories flooded his mind. He clearly recalled every detail of their meeting and the circumstances which led to its sitting on his sill. It was a five inch tall Angel figurine with outstretched wings. It came into his possession one magical day many years ago... the day he met and lost Cynthia

While walking in the forest one sunny September afternoon, he came upon a small clearing where a deer was quietly grazing. He stopped to marvel at its grace and beauty. It did not seem to mind his presence. Then he saw her. She sat against a large oak tree, to the left of the little meadow, smiling at him with the same expression of wonder on her face he had on his while watching the deer. She spoke with a voice so soft, so enchanting, he had the impression it brushed his cheek like a passing butterfly.

"She will not bolt. We have been enjoying each other's company for some time. We both welcome you to our little sanctuary on this glorious day."

Rob felt a rush of warmth flow up his spine. "I'm enchanted. Hello! My name is Rob. I am very pleased to meet you. I don't believe I have ever come upon a more breath taking scene in all my short life."

"I am called Cynthia and I am pleased to make your acquaintance young Rob", she said in a disarmingly charming voice.

This conversation seemed a little curious to Rob, who was unaccustomed to running into any women alone in the forest. Cynthia was very attractive and amiable. Most women Rob had met would not be caught dead out here alone, not to mention carrying on a conversation with a complete stranger. Although he was very pleasantly surprised at the whole scene, he could not help but think it rather odd.

"You seem to be quite at home in the forest, Cynthia. What brings you out here?" He said affably, moving with calculated, measured steps, so as not to startle the deer or this remarkable young lady.

"Yes," she answered with a smile so sweet it could have caused his teeth to ache. "I feel quite at home wherever I am. The forest and her creatures are most delightful company. Come. Join me here under this tree. I believe we have much to discuss," she gestured to him invitingly.

As much as he may have hoped otherwise, he could not find any sexual connotation in her gesture. Rob was delighted with her openness and lack of fear, nonetheless. 'Such a gentle, trusting soul' he thought to himself as he sat down beside her under the tree.

Rob was enchanted by her peculiar choice of terminology, almost as if she was unfamiliar with modern English. She spoke about how she felt humans were falling short of their potential and how easily they forgot where they originated. At the time, Rob was just so enchanted by her that he was not paying a whole lot of attention to the content of her dialogue. The truth was, he was having difficulty following her train of thought. He was more interested in her mannerisms and the charming way she spoke. His memories of that day were dominated by elegant visual images of her beauty and grace and the euphonious sound of her voice.

After only a few minutes he began to feel very comfortable in her presence. He could not recall ever having felt this close to any human being before, not even with his own mother. He had the strangest impression he had known her for many lifetimes, even though he had never given reincarnation much thought. It seemed unimaginable she would not always be there.

Although he participated in the conversation, a greater part of him was lost in his own thoughts and feelings about her. In spite of the fact that she was probably the most attractive woman he ever met, his feelings for her leaned more toward those of a brother. His thoughts ran along the lines of 'I could fall in love with a woman like her.' He found the whole dialogue in his mind rather confusing. Lucky for him Cynthia talked almost non stop and didn't seem to notice he was so lost in his head he missed large chunks of her dialogue.

As dusk began to settle in, Rob asked her if she would like to accompany him to his place for a bite to eat. It was close by and afterwards they could go for a stroll down to the lake and watch the moonrise. To his surprise, she agreed and they stretched their legs for the walk to town.

Sitting there, enchanted and bewildered, he hadn't noticed that his legs had fallen asleep. They had to wait a few minutes for the blood to start circulating again. The shadows were getting deeper now, so they broke into a swift stride in order to clear the woods before it got too dark to see where they were going.

When they arrived at his apartment, he immediately began foraging about in his fridge to see what he could make that was edible. Normally he just slapped something together. Eating was not one of the priorities in his life. He ate because he had to. But this time he wanted to impress her with something special.

After checking out his place and its contents she came toward the kitchenette and leaned casually in the doorway. She watched him silently as he fumbled around the kitchen like a lost dog at a birthday party. He was excited but when he became aware of her in the doorway he thought, 'She must think I'm a klutz. I really don't know what I'm doing and she knows it!'

"Rob, relax. Cooking is not an activity I have ever engaged in. I think you are doing fine but then what do I know of such things?" she said half jokingly. Rob thought it a rather odd remark but didn't give it much thought. He was too busy being uncomfortable.

She didn't seem to eat any of whatever it was he cooked. He thought it tasted pretty good but she wasn't touching it. He was only faintly aware his ego was having difficulty with it. He was so deeply engrossed in her enthusiasm; he eventually forgot to be self-conscious.

After they finished supper, he put the leftovers in the fridge and the dishes in the sink, then they went out for a walk to the lake. It was a small lake, more like a large puddle, in the center of town. There was a raft built, about fifty feet out from the shore, with a slide on it, where the town's folk spent their hot summer days cooling off. The beach was small because the waters edge, at this part of the lake, dropped off suddenly to a depth of fifteen feet only a few yards from shore.

16

A pathway circled the lake, which was only sparsely populated with residences. The main feature was a park behind the beach where the town had reassembled the old church rectory (after careful disassembly) when the priests decided they needed a new home beside the church, two blocks away. The old three story stone structure now housed a museum on the upper two floors and changing rooms in the basement for beach-goers in summer and skaters in the winter.

The forested mountain, on the east side of town, served as a backdrop and the western sky was as clear and brilliantly lit by a full moon as any Hollywood movie set. The moonlight, shimmering off the softly rippling surface of the lake, set the mood for a fine conversation.

"This mountain is an extinct volcano," Rob said, trying to lighten the conversation. "There are seven old crater lakes up there and each one is stocked with a different species of fish. The Catholic Church up until a few years ago owned the whole mountain. The monks stocked the lakes and built miles of trails upon which to walk while meditating. In my teen years I spent a lot of time wondering those hills, rafting, fishing and camping out with my friends. Now that I'm working, I don't find much time to go up on the mountain and enjoy those activities that gave me so much pleasure in my youth.

The wind had died down and the surface of the water was as smooth as glass. Cynthia threw a pebble into the lake. The ripples spread rapidly, shattering the reflection of the moon. "All it takes is one person to step beyond the confines of conventional thought to shatter the illusion and influence the collective consciousness of the entire species."

"I would just like to step beyond my own limiting thoughts to something different but I don't know what that might look like or how to get there," Rob said without much emotion. He always thought there must be more to life than what he was experiencing but he had no idea what it might be. "I have been doing a lot of reading on a variety of subjects but I feel like a prisoner of this cultural system and my own emotional makeup."

"Believe me, Rob, you are on the right track. You will just have to cultivate patience because eventually you will understand what has been hidden from you."

The night air was beginning to chill so they decided to return to his apartment to continue their conversation. They talked into the wee hours of the morning. Somewhere in the night he faded into a deep, dreamless sleep. He awoke with a start, around eight thirty, to see her standing calmly by the door with a mischievous smile on her face.

"Oh my God. Don't tell me I fell asleep on you!" He jumped up from the floor, stumbled and fell onto the couch. He tried to recover his composure but it was too late. She was already doubled over with laughter. Her laugh was so charming he finally gave in and joined her in the moment.

"I bet it did look pretty goofy," he said with the rye smile.

"Actually, I found it quite delightful," she offered. "I have truly enjoyed our time together but I am afraid I have to go now. Here. I want you to have this." She stretched out her right arm and handed him the angel figurine. "Get in touch with your Angel, Rob. She is waiting to help you discover more about yourself," and without further ado she turned, walked out never to return.

The abruptness of her departure left Rob stunned for quite a while. He had no idea what she meant or why she left without telling him where he could contact her again. He sat in his room and stared at the walls dumbfounded for days. Every night for weeks he went over every detail he could recall but he could never figure out what actually happened or why he never got her phone number. Eventually he went back to living the way he always had - without much enthusiasm.

Although he dated occasionally, none of these women could come close to the image he held in his mind of Cynthia. After a few years he even gave up dating altogether. Instead, he lost himself in his job and TV. He even lost his interest in reading.

A Really Big Surprise

Now Rob was ready to leave his apartment. He sold or gave away most of his stuff. He planned to travel light but he was drawn to the angel figurine on the windowsill. It was as if it was calling to him to be taken along for the ride.

He reached out to pick her up and felt an old familiar sensation rush up his spine. He also noticed there was no dust on her and she seemed to be glowing ever so slightly. He picked her up, hesitantly, between his fingers.

There was a bright flash and everything disappeared. As his sight returned, he saw Cynthia standing in front of him!

"It's about time, Rob" she exclaimed with the same mischievous smile she had the morning she left.

"Cynthia!?" he gasped.

"Yes. I have been waiting patiently all these years for you to reach out to me, Rob." Her smile was as charming and disarming as ever.

"I don't get it", he mumbled as he looked around. They were in a very bright place with no defining characteristics - no objects, corners, shadows or lines. All he could make out was Cynthia - with a large pair of outstretched wings! 'This is most disorienting indeed', he thought.

In obvious response to his state of confusion she softly said, "No, Rob. You have not died and gone to heaven. This is the dwelling place of your soul. Actually, this is not a place at all, at least not in the usual way you think of places. And I don't want you to be alarmed by the fact that you have no body here."

He looked down. "No kidding!" He looked back at Cynthia. "How is it you do?"

"I don't," she said as a matter of fact. "I am appearing to you in this form so you can have a point of reference - the last object of your attention before you came here." Her voice was calm, deliberate and purposefully conversational.

He was aware she was doing everything to assure him and make him feel comfortable in this new environment. He appreciated the way she could do that. He was starting to get a grip on his panic.

"So, if neither of us has a body, how can we be talking?" he asked not quite sure how to relate to any of this situation.

"There are more ways to communicate than with just talk, silly. You know this but you have blocked it out, haven't you? In our last encounter we did not speak either." she was almost teasing in her reproach.

Rob was even more confused. "I remember we talked for almost ten hours"

"Well you are partly right. We did converse for a long time but the entire conversation took place on a completely different level. You call it telepathy in your reality. Here, it is the only way we communicate. It is the only way I can communicate with you in any reality you might find yourself in. And you are beginning to suspect there is far more to reality than you formally thought," she said with a wink - a very familiar wink!

"You are referring to the exploding TV incident, I suppose" he only half asked, suddenly remembering why she looked so familiar at the time.

"Yes. We decided it was time to give you a wake up call. You had become so stuck in your life you forgot what you came to the Earth plane to accomplish," she said in her best impression of a reproachful schoolteacher but she could not keep up the act. She finally broke out in a big smile.

"Whoa! Step back for a minute here, sister. Who are 'we' and what do you mean I came to Earth. What am I, a space alien with amnesia or something?" He was almost beginning to loose his composure again.

"No, you are not an alien. Well, at least not the way you normally think of aliens. You see, you came to Earth from a different plane of existence and you did forget where you came from, but those are the rules of the game in physical reality. If you remembered all the lives your soul has ever experienced in third dimensional reality, you would be so confused you would not be able to function. You have become so confused, as it is, you can barely function now.

"The 'we' I referred to are myself, your personal angel (with this she executed a deep curtsy) and your soul or higher self, as some prefer to call it. We became concerned about your ego frittering away your life". She had the schoolteacher look of disapproval again but it faded into a grin very quickly.

"Angel, huh!" Rob was not sure what he thought of that.

"Well, I am a guide who has volunteered to help you find your way home. I have no physical form so I don't really have wings. I appear to you in this form because I thought you might accept it easier. Besides, I rather enjoy appearing as an angel. I suites my personality, don't you think?"

"It certainly is the impression of you that I have carried with me all these years," Rob said, almost embarrassed to admit it to her.

"When you were a child, you believed you had a guardian angel. Later you thought your angel had abandoned you. I wanted you to know I have never abandoned you Rob. You just abandoned your belief in angels." Her voice had no tone of condemnation in it.

Rob was, again, becoming a little perplexed. "Let me get this straight. I'm not an alien but I come from a different place to accomplish something on this planet but I forgot what it was.

Then I abandoned my belief in angels when..." He hesitated for a moment.

"When those around you said your belief was childish nonsense. The fact is, you do have spiritual guides who accompany you to the Earth plane and you are aware of their presence at birth. It is sad but because those around you have forgotten the presence of their guides, they try to get you to forget yours too. It is a tragedy that has been going on for thousands of years.

"All humans come to life with a purpose. You all chose the Earth plane because of the richness of possible experiences. There is no other way for the soul to delight in the physical sensations of touch, smell, taste, sight and sound. What incredible gifts!" she sighed. "Even angels envy what most humans take for granted. It is a terrible shame, this lack of appreciation we witness among you.

"Our job is to reach out to you, to try to awaken a remembering of your origins and the reason you chose this life."

"You reached out to me? I'm the one who picked you up!" he said with a mixture of perplexity and mild indignation.

"Do you remember the day we met in the forest and I gave you the angel figurine?" Her voice was as soothing as chicken soup when you have a cold.

"Ah, yes" he said, not quite sure what the connection could be.

"This is complicated but I will try to explain it to you in a way you might understand. I was never a human but I appeared to you in that form to give you the figurine so you could contact me when you were ready. I was not real, at least not in the physical sense. That is why I never came back - although I have been by your side since you were born.

"You see, angels are allowed to appear on occasion but we cannot experience physical reality. This is why I had to remain as an inanimate object, so one day you could pick me up. Then I could bring you here. I could not interfere with your free will. I had to wait until you decided you were ready.

"And yes," she read his mind, "that is why, although you were enchanted by the way I appeared to you, you had no sexual feelings toward me. Then, as now, we were communicating on a non-physical level. Your sexual feelings are a purely physical response to those living in physical form, or - in the case of necrophiliacs - the dead, but that is another matter altogether and I'm not quite sure what to make of it."

"You and me both. But thanks for clearing the sexual thing up for me. I was wondering why the most beautiful woman I ever met didn't turn me on. For a while I thought I was impotent.

"By the way, I don't recall having decided to come here. How could I when I didn't even know this place existed?"

"You did it indirectly, I suppose. You expressed a desire to know more about Truth and the nature of reality. You did decide to change and seek a new way of experiencing your life. Well... here you are!" She threw up her wings and looked around as if to say 'What do you think of it so far?'

"Do you mean I have to spend the rest of my life is this place? No offense. You may be beautiful and all but I was hoping to have a few more of those physical experiences you say angels envy so much."

"Rob, Rob, Rob." She wagged her finger at him in mock disappointment. "You still don't get it. This is not your life. This is your soul. Time does not exist here. In your terms, this will only seem like a second of your time."

"Oh. That's a relief. Then, what are we doing here?"

"After the TV's demise, you expressed a need to get in touch with the real you. Do you remember saying 'If this isn't real then what is? Is there more to me than I previously thought?'

This is the real you. This is your true Self. This is where you reside. The life you have on the Earth plane is more or less a dream your soul is having in order to gain a broader perspective of reality."

"Do you mean I am just a dream?" He tried to pinch himself to check if he was real or not but couldn't find his body. "Are you saying the soul is not all knowing or complete?" He rarely thought about religious matters but he felt the soul was akin to god in omnipotence.

"No. Your present personality is real but there is far more to you than just your physical body. Your soul lives

25

more than just one physical lifetime in its quest for more knowledge. The Earth plane is a school of sorts, where the soul tries to expand its awareness so it can find its way home. Not even what you call god is a static entity. In fact, what you call god is not the creator of all you see but is actually a creation of humanity but I will explain that later. Everything in creation is in a constant state of becoming, growing and expanding."

"Wait a minute. Are you saying that the being that created the Universe is still in a process of learning new stuff? Hold the phone, here, momma! This blows the lid off a whole new can of worms." His juices were starting to flow now.

"There is an inherent intelligence in everything that exists, including rocks, planets, solar systems and galaxies. The All That Is created all this to expand Its own self awareness through the experiences of every aspect of Its creation."

"You have got to be kidding! Are you trying to tell me there is no angry God who sits in judgment over everything we say and do?" Rob looked around to see if a bolt of lightning was coming toward them.

"Yes. That god is only a creation of humans who had forgotten their own divinity. It exists, it thrives, on the energy people feed it through their thoughts and beliefs. It has become a kind of psychic vampire, feeding on their energy. It feels secure that people are too frightened to stop believing in it. If they did, it would cease to exist in a millisecond."

"Holy shit!" Rob was getting even more nervous about this kind of blasphemous talk. Although he was not religious by nature, there were certain things one did not

26

say out loud concerning god. He kept looking over his shoulder, expecting divine wrath to strike them both down.

"This is stepping on some very dangerous ground. Some godly noses may get out of joint here!"

"Oh, Rob, settle down. Nobody is going to zap you for hearing the truth" she tried to assure him.

"The truth! The truth! What you are telling me not only stretches the boundary of accepted truth, it down right says it has all been a colossal lie! Excuse me if I seem a little incredulous, here but even after all I have experienced today, I am still having trouble swallowing this god stuff. I realize there is far more to reality than is commonly accepted but you are asking a bit much of me here."

She looked deeply concerned and perplexed at his reluctance to accept what she was trying to tell him. "Rob, brace yourself. That is not all there is to say on this matter."

Rob looked for a place to hide without success. "W... what do you mean?" he asked sheepishly.

"There is more than one of these man made gods."

"There is?" He wasn't sure it was safe to hang out with this being anymore.

"There are several gods, all created by the major religions and all exist within your planetary sphere, all feeding off human energy - energy which is produced by human fear and suffering. These gods were not part of the plan for your experience here but because you were given free will, the unexpected is what happened."

"OK then. Who is in charge here? I mean, if god is a figment of our imagination, who do you represent? Who gives you your orders?"

"Nobody gives me orders. I volunteered for this job because it is my nature. Angels - or guiding spirits, if you prefer, come from the original dwelling place of souls. The souls who are experiencing lifetimes on the Earth plane were lost a long time ago when they decided to break ranks with the original order of things. They chose to leave home in search of new experiences and got lost. They have been trying to find their way home ever since.

"The being you call Earth is a very old soul, who volunteered to come into this realm to provide a dwelling place for these lost souls and to provide a place where they could evolve and remember their way back to heaven."

"Heaven? Do you mean we are all struggling to get to the place where we sit on clouds and play harps?" He always thought it would be an awfully boring ordeal.

"No." She said with infinite patience. "Heaven is the original home of souls. Even if I took you there, I do not think you would be able to absorb the intensity or the immensity of it. Your soul, however, does remember heaven. As a physical being, you can fathom the immensity of your physical universe. This is the reality you operate in, so it is where you need to focus your attention."

"Oh! Oh! Before we go much further, I have to know the answer to the question that is burning a hole in everybody's brain these days. Are we alone in the Universe or are there others like us living on other planets?"

"Human's are the only species who experience life as you know it. Life on other planets will exist when you are ready to accept it. What you think of as physical life does not exist outside your conscious awareness. It is only when you bring it into your awareness that it exists in your third dimensional reality. This can only happen if both parties agree to acknowledge each other's existence on the subconscious level.

"What most humans have trouble understanding is there are a multitude of plains of existence where reality is experienced in a variety of different ways which are beyond your present capacity to comprehend. Even on the Earth plain, there are millions of different ways to experience reality. Every aspect of your reality has consciousness. A rock is aware of its own life force. They are not inanimate objects. Their energy vibrates at a different rate than yours does, so it is very difficult to tune into their frequency. There are those among you, particularly among cultures which practice shamanism, who can tune their energy output in such a way it allows them to communicate with rocks, as well as many other forms of life."

"Yes, I have heard of such things. Why is it we, in our society, do not know how to do these things?" he asked but he suspected he already knew the answer.

"The reason your culture does not is because you were never taught to. It is not an accepted part of your culture's experience. Rocks have a consciousness and The All That Is is aware of it. This is true of billions of forms of existence you cannot perceive."

"Right!" He would have given her an incredulous look except, at this point in time, he didn't have a face. "I can't say I don't get the general drift of what you are saying but this does stretch the boundaries of accepted belief systems to the Max, don't you think?"

"Yes. This is because belief systems, like the human capacity to think, are rather limited."

"Are you insinuating we are not as intelligent as we think we are?" he interjected.

"No. I am trying to say the brain is not the seat of your intelligence. You have created belief systems to attempt to make sense of what was beyond the capacity of your brain to understand. The brain is a useful tool but in order to have real understanding you must learn to listen to your heart. The soul speaks to you through your hearts, not your brains. This is why you find yourselves rather confused about the nature of reality.

"Humans have become preoccupied with their physical senses. There is an environmental crisis on your planet because you have forgotten how to listen to your hearts, to your inner guidance."

"Do you mean the environment is suffering from our inability to connect with our souls and not from pollution?"

"Partly. What you call pollution is a physical manifestation of your confusion and pain. Your inability to connect with the source of your divine energy has left you with illness and suffering. The Earth is dying because She was never meant to hold the weight of so many heavy, thick beings. Your energy is so dense from your total focus on your physical senses it is crushing your Mother Earth.

"You are, essentially, light beings who have forgotten why you are on the Earth plain, in the first place. In forgetting, you have become more and more physical and therefore more dense. Earth is a sentient light being too but She is suffering from your physical weight. You have been inflicting terrible pain on her body because of your need to fill the black hole you have created by shutting yourself off from the source of love offered to you by your soul."

"That is horrible. I had no idea we were inflicting such pain on her. Hell, I didn't know she could feel pain!"

"Yes. She is a conscious, sentient being, after all. But she has boundless love for you. She is willing to make the sacrifice, if needed. But this was not her original intention. Because she is in such a weakened state, we have come to assist in the process of awakening. We have come, not only to help mankind out of its present predicament, but to save the life of our dear sister as well."

"I don't get it. If we are such a burden to the Earth, why doesn't she do something about us? Why doesn't she just scratch us off like a dog would a flea? Wait a minute. Is that what all the increase in volcanic activity, hurricanes, tornadoes and flooding is about? Is she pissed off?"

"No. Those things are a result of your impact on Her. She is not causing these activities. You have to also realize many of you are expecting these things to happen. The belief that there should be some sort of divine retribution for the failings of mankind to adhere to "God's Law" is also partly responsible. Those who believe in divine retribution are putting out a tremendous amount of energy in that direction. It is time to wake up from your slumber and remember why you decided to be born in the first place."

"Why do we choose to be born into physical reality?"

"Each person has their own reasons. You choose the circumstances of your life in order to work through certain life experiences that will expand your perspective of life through the richness and diversity of sensations and possibilities. This is intended to add to your spiritual growth."

"Slow down a minute here. You are going a little too fast! I thought spiritual growth was about going off into a cave to contemplate our navels for years on end or how well we adhere to a particular set of religious doctrines."

"No. Spiritual growth has more to do with living ones life consciously. It is your experiences that assist your soul in the process of broadening its perspective. Sitting in a cave is avoiding life."

"I'm a little disillusioned by this whole spiritual bit. I mean, I have heard a lot of people give lip service to 'spiritual growth' but in the end all they wanted was my money or they used their illusion of spirituality to get some naive young lady in the sack."

"It is not only men who play that game," she corrected him. "Poor Rob. You have been hanging out with the wrong crowd again, haven't you?" she mocked him by pouting. "But you are right. There are very few who have any clarity on the subject. Those who do don't usually feel a need to go around telling others about it. It is also very difficult to find the truth among the thousands of different belief systems that abound on your world. Most contain the seeds of truth but most fall short because the truth cannot be found in words. It can only be found through your personal connection to the wisdom of your soul and your experiences of life."

"No wonder I'm so confused!" Rob interjected, "I don't even have a life and I wasn't even aware I could communicate with my soul. How was I supposed to find the truth?"

"The point most people miss is that the truth is only relevant to the beholder. You can only find it within yourself and it can only make sense to you. Everything everybody else is trying to pass off as truth is just their opinion of what they think the truth is. Unfortunately, most people only parrot what somebody else told them because very few take the time to look within. If you want to find the truth, listen to the guidance of your heart. It will never steer you in the wrong direction or ask anything of you."

"Ya! Right! Why is it every relationship I've had, seemed to only bring pain or disappointment with it? Why have all the great loves of my life turned into nightmares?"

"Most of the time you make decisions based on thinking about the consequences of your actions - if they will benefit you or not. Decision-making is a vice. If you trusted your gut instinct - your inner guidance - you would do what is right for all concerned. In the long run, it is what is best for you, too.

"As for falling in love, if you think about it, you will realize you were 'falling' more for the fantasy than the person. You were trying to get that person to fill up the empty space in your life that is yours to fill. You cannot be in love with someone. You can only be in a state of Love. Some refer to it as being in a state of Grace.

"Love is what creates everything. You are Love. If you reopen your connection to your soul, you will find you are surrounded by the same boundless, Loving energy that creates universes - all the time. It is you who have closed yourselves off from the source of Love. Once you can break free of the confining prison of your social conditioning, you will be able to open you heart and reconnect to your soul. Then you will have all the love you can possibly need. You can share your love with another but you cannot create a state of love with someone. You are either in it or you are not."

"This is confusing. I thought love was generated by two people who came together through mutual admiration or some mysterious 'chemistry' that binds them to each other."

"This mysterious 'chemistry', as you call it, is a cocktail of hormones produced in your brain called endorphins. The whole process of 'falling in love' is more of a cerebral exercise than a heart condition. It fulfills a need but it is not love. Real love comes from a heart that is open to the infinite Love offered to you by your soul. If you are in a state of Grace, balance and harmony within yourself and your environment, Love comes to you. It can only be reached by listening to and acting on the knowing of ones heart.

"But it is rare for people to listen because they are too busy paying attention to the constant babble of their ego - or ignoring it."

"What is that supposed to mean?" Rob asked, a little agitated by the direction this was heading.

"The inner chatter that continually drones on like a broken record in your heads. Your ego is in a constant state of agitation, continually talking to itself. If you listen carefully to the conversation, you will hear a disjointed ramble of statements or half statements based on beliefs about life which were handed to you by those around you."

"Well, yes. I have paid attention to the noise in my head on occasion. A lot of the time it is either reminding me what a screwed up person I am or it is plotting how to manipulate others for what I can get from them." This was a most depressing thought for Rob. Part of him thought he had been basically a good person but this particular view of himself was very discouraging. It was one of the reasons he had slowly curtailed his contact with other people. It was an aspect of himself that disgusted him. "I would really like to know how to turn this sucker off!"

"It is not about turning it off so much as it is about reprogramming the dialogue, Rob." Cynthia looked around, and then stooped down as if she were picking something up. She held out her hand. In it was a compact ball of dirt.

Rob looked around. They were still in this place of no defining characteristics. "Where did you get that?" he asked without expecting an answer.

"Anything is possible but that discussion is for another time and place. For now I wanted to illustrate a point. This ball of dirt represents the egos conversation with itself. It is extremely compact and limiting in its perspective and range." She then crumbled it in her hand and scattered it about them with a broad sweep of her arm. "That is the wisdom of your heart which you have been ignoring."

Up on the Roof

Rob and Cynthia were now standing on top of a very high building overlooking a large city. Below, from their vantage point, he could see thousands of people scurrying about like tiny insects. The change in perspective caught him off guard. Rob stumbled and nearly fell over the edge but Cynthia touched his shoulder and he regained his balance.

"Thanks," he said, visibly shaken by the sudden change of venue. "Is there anybody on Earth who actually listens to their hearts?"

"Yes." she said as a matter of fact.

"Do they know what the truth is, then?"

"Only their own."

"Then why are they not trying to wake us up?"

She leaned forward and looked down on the crowd as if looking for an answer, straightened up and looked at Rob. "There have been those who have tried without much success. Most don't feel a need to go around telling others about it."

"That doesn't make sense. I look around at those I know and it looks to me like we are all drowning out here. We seem to be in dire need of a little help. Where is their compassion?" Rob found himself looking down at the street below with a mixed sense of pity, concern and sorrow, mostly for himself.

"It is not a matter of compassion. Very few understand the true meaning of compassion. The common perception of the word is wrought with a sense of guilt and duty. The fact is, nobody can help anybody unless a person asks for it and is ready to accept it. You have to realize you have a problem for which you are seeking a solution. Only then are you willing to accept help. If someone tells you you have a problem and they can help you with it, you will automatically write them off as an interfering twit. It is in your nature.

"Many of those who feel a need to expound upon their views do so because they are either uncertain of their beliefs and need others to validate them or their egos are insecure and need to impress others with their persona of cleverness. Neither have any sense of who they are. They have no real connection to their souls. They also give people with right intent a bad name.

"Those who are certain of their truth know it is only relevant to them. They do not need external validation or to impress anybody. They know others need to come to their own understanding in their own way, without interference. It is up to every individual to make the decision to break free of his or her prison. They created it. They have to tear down the walls "

"Do you mean that if I find the truth I cannot share it?" There went Rob's fleeting fantasy of becoming the next messiah.

"The only way to share your truth in any way others might comprehend would be for you to become your truth. You cannot help anybody unless they decide it is time to wake up."

"That is an elusive concept!" He wasn't quite sure what she was getting at.

"To become your truth, you incorporate what you have learned into how you live your life. When you break free of your prison, you will radiate the love that is yours for the asking. Others will seek to know what it is you have found. You will then understand just what and if they are ready to hear." She sat down on the edge of the roof and settled into what seemed was going to be a long explanation.

"Knowledge is a powerful force for good but a little knowledge is dangerous, as the old saying goes. The ego, because of its limited capacity for real understanding, will try to manipulate others to get what it wants. You only have to look to your political and religious leaders to see how the ego's limited understanding of power can corrupt intention."

Rob smiled at this remark. "Yes. That is pretty obvious," he said with a note of sarcasm.

"Don't be so quick to judge others, Rob. Don't forget that everybody has been indoctrinated into the same set of limiting beliefs about reality as you have. All humans are working and struggling through life with the same set of handicaps."

"How did things get so..." Rob searched for the right word.

"Confused?" she interjected. "It is difficult to relate thousands of your years of decline," she said, with a note of sadness. "You are stuck in physical reality because of commonly held beliefs about it. There have also been those among you who have had a vested interest in keeping the truth of your real potential from you. They have been deceived by their own delusions of power. They see themselves as the guardians of the faith but they have long forgotten the truth in their own lives. Power cannot be gained from without or by the subjugation of others. Real power comes from a full awareness of your own divinity. If everyone knew about and was able to access the knowledge of their souls, there would be no need for governments or religions. Everybody would respect the divine in all creatures and act accordingly."

"But what about the organizational aspect of governments and society? Who would feed all these people? How would anything get done? What would be the motivation to go to work and pay the bills?" He thought he had her on this one.

"If you fully understood your capacity for creativity, you would not need jobs, money or bills. All you ever need is offered to you by your soul. What you don't understand is that you create everything you perceive and experience in your life by manifesting your thoughts and beliefs. It will take discipline to control your thoughts so your needs are met. This is a vital piece of the puzzle which could free humanity from the bondage of the myth of victimhood."

"No kidding!" Rob looked down at the throngs. "I've felt like a victim of circumstance all my life. What you are saying takes what I've heard to a whole new level. You realize, however, this will be a very hard sell down there," as he pointed at the street below. "Nobody is going to want to accept they are creating cancer, starvation or plane crashes. I don't think they will want to accept that kind of responsibility, do you?"

"No but think about this. Most people create their lives by default. Most go on repeating old belief and thought patterns without realizing they are repeating the same old patterns of experience. These events may come in different disguises - places, names, times, etcetera - but the patterns are the same. Basically, it's like stubbing the same toe on different objects. By taking responsibility for and control over your thoughts and what they manifest, you will remove those obstacles to a more fulfilling life experience."

"I can almost see the possibilities," he spoke in a soft, pensive voice, "but how do we overcome our old patterns of reacting to life if it is all we know?"

"It is not easy to overcome a life time of habitual thinking. First you have to become conscious of your thoughts. Given your penchant for ignoring your inner dialogue, this may be easier said than done but it is the first step toward self awareness. The second is to become aware of the results your thoughts bring into your life. If you don't like the results, then you can make the conscious effort to change the old patterns of thought by replacing them with new ones that will produce the desired outcomes. This takes discipline and time."

"I can see how people are going to have a lot of trouble with this discipline thing. Most people, including myself, would consider it a real brain drain." Rob said, shaking his head from side to side. "So what does time have to do with it if it doesn't exist?"

"I didn't say it didn't exist. I said it only existed in your reality. You guys invented it so it exists for you. It will take time to recognize the old thought patterns and the repeated results. You have had your habit of thinking for all of your life, so you will not be able to just change it over night. You have come to know you are eternal, so time is relative. It may take a few years or a few lifetimes. It depends on how strong your determination and focus are. Eventually you will be able to shift your focus on a consistent basis until joy becomes the dominant effect in your life."

"Now there's a concept but I'm not even sure what I want or what would make me happy. I know what I don't want and that is what I usually get, more often than not."

"That is what most people know - what they don't want. By focusing on it, though, it is what they manifest."

Rob gave her a questioning look. "I'm not sure I like the sound of this." He struggled with the idea for a moment. He began to feel a real conflict inside. His old beliefs were jockeying for position. Finally he had enough and shouted, "Stop!" His mind became quiet. 'Now this is more like it,' he thought. "So if I can just imagine what I want, I can have it?"

"Yes!" she said with certainty, then she cautioned, "as long as you are not imposing your will on another."

"What if I want to have a wonderful sexual relationship with a woman?"

"If your intent resonates with your true self and it feels like a joyful union when you visualize it, she will come into your life. Like attracts like, so you will not be imposing anything on her because she will have the same intent."

"What if I want pots of money?" Rob asked cautiously, always having felt there was something dirty about the stuff.

"With clear intent and focus you can have everything you want. The reason you are not getting it now is you keep contradicting your desire with your belief there is something selfish about what you want."

"That is a pretty scary thought!"

"Why?"

"Selfishness is frowned upon in our society and what you are saying sounds pretty selfish to me. Besides, how can I keep my thoughts from contradicting my wishes?" Bob knew how hard it was to keep track of which part of him was in control at any given time.

"You are all you have. Each person is the creator of his or her own reality. Only people, who are alike, in some way, will be attracted into each other's reality. If you look at the people and situations you are attracting into your life, you will have a pretty clear indication of where you are, mentally and emotionally, in any given moment. If you want sympathy and validation for your suffering, you will find no shortage of support. If you are happy and centered in yourself, you will attract joyful people. If you are grateful for life and the abundance inherent in it, you will be abundant."

"Misery loves company, eh! This sounds a little too simple to me." Rob's skepticism reared its ugly head.

"It is simple. This is why it escapes most people. You have been trained since birth to complicate the heck out of everything. You cannot buy happiness. Nobody can bring it to you. It cannot be found outside yourself. You have to manifest it by making the connection to the source your number one priority. This is what is meant by Self Love. You are far more than the confines of your body or your ego and its petty wants and desires. Without a connection to the source, loving energy cannot flow to you or from you.

The only power you can have is in the creation of your own reality. The only responsibility you have is in how you experience that reality. If you understood the only law governing life is karma, then you would be inclined to do only good deeds because it is the only way you can be happy."

What exactly do you mean by karma? I have heard a lot of different interpretations of it. Which ones are you referring to?" Rob inquired.

"For every action there is an equal and opposite reaction. You get back out of life what you put into it," Cynthia responded.

The Socially Conditioned Mind

Cynthia began to beat her wings rapidly, creating a wind that pushed against Rob's eyes. He shut them instinctively. When he reopened them they were standing in a room where several men sat quietly reading their newspapers. Judging by the decor of the room, they seemed to be in an exclusive men's club. Although he could see they were not talking, he could distinctly hear several voices coming from their direction.

"What am I going to do about Donny? He doesn't want to go to college... That prick Harry has been gloating over his new Lexus all day. If I close the Bradford deal, I'll get the Jaguar I've been looking at and he can shove his Lexus where the sun don't shine... It's Harriet's birthday next week. I had better get her a gift or I won't here the end of it... The new girl in billing is some nice piece of merchandise. I wonder if I can charm the pants off of her... God, I don't know where I'm going to get the time to see the doctor about this blood in my urine... I'm really getting tired of that weasel Donavon. If he brings in the Ford contract, he will make me look bad with upper management..."

"What the heck is going on here?" Rob looked over at Cynthia standing to his left. "Are we ease dropping on their thoughts, or something?"

"Yes. I wanted you to see the socially conditioned mind in action. I wanted you to know your ego is not who you are. When you came into this body, you were wise, compassionate and filled with love. But those around you had forgotten where they came from and all the gifts they came to their lives with. They looked upon you as an empty vessel that needed to be filled because this is how they were treated when they arrived. In other words, your mind was socially conditioned by other socially conditioned minds. Those minds had long ago forgotten who they were.

"You arrived on Earth to bring love and light back into their lives. They felt it was their duty to raise you in the tradition they were raised in, not knowing the roles were reversed. What they gave you was a continuation of a millennia old lie about the nature of reality based on fear and suffering. You created your ego out of self defense.

"You must remember this. Compared to your place of origin, combined with your relative helplessness when you arrived, the Earth plain seemed like a hostile environment. Because you were so physically dependent on your caregivers, you trusted them implicitly to teach you about your new circumstances. You forgot you came to teach them.

"In the process of imparting their 'knowledge' to you, they also passed on their combined neuroses. Your entire childhood was spent absorbing all the psychic rubble of those adults around you. Their beliefs about love, life and reality were twisted by thousands of years of focus on material existence without an understanding of the true nature of their connection to spirit.

"The feeling of separation you feel is the cause of all the pain and suffering humans have inflicted upon themselves and everything around them all this time.

"You are, first and foremost, a spiritual being. Your physical body and socially conditioned mind are but tiny aspects of a much greater entity that is your source of love and creative energy. Your soul is not an aspect of you. You are an aspect of your soul. Your soul is not emotionally attached to your experiences of life. It does not sit in judgment of your actions. There is no good, bad or indifference as far as it is concerned.

"Your soul is constantly sending you loving energy. Without a sense of connection to it or even an understanding of its true nature and intent, you cannot receive love. This is the simple truth and tragedy of your lives - you don't even know the nature of your relationship with your soul. Nobody informed you because nobody informed them and now nobody remembers."

He looked around the room at the men who sat reading their papers. A deep sense of their isolation from each other triggered his own feelings of isolation and he began to weep from the intense sorrow welling up from the pit of his stomach.

"God, I wish I hadn't agreed to go to the opera with Jean. I should work on the Paterson file tonight... Bobby needs braces and there just isn't enough money in my budget to buy them... Tomorrow I must remember to look up the prospectus on those stocks I would like to purchase... If I get one more moron coming to me with stupid proposals, I will shoot him and call it a mercy killing... How am I going to get away for that fishing trip with Harry and James..? Where am I going to get the cash for the new carpet Joyce keeps pestering me for..."

Rob couldn't tell if the voices were coming from his head or theirs. "Please get me out of here. I can't take any more of this pain!" he sobbed.

She put her arm around his shoulders to console him. "Rob, you need to see and feel this. This is how your mind keeps you stuck in this false reality. You need this impetus to motivate you to make some radical changes in the way you live your life.

"Life presents to you exactly what you ask for and what you believe you deserve. Your soul wants you to be happy but it is not attached to your actions. Whether you enjoy your life or not does not effect how much your soul loves you. You are its creation. What matters to it is whether or not you learn from your experiences. The point is to become aware you are creating your life and take total responsible for your experience.

"This is an opportunity to change how you create your reality because in this new self awareness, you know your connectedness and your conscious participation in the process of creation. You will no longer be trapped in physical reality. You will no longer be a victim of circumstance."

"But I have done the victim so well!" Rob said with a sense of terminal victimness. "I'm almost afraid to let it go. It has become such an integral part of my identity - a comfortable place to be. I mean, it is painful but comfortable in a familiar sort of way. What will become of me if I let go of my identity?"

"Do you think, after all you have witnessed, that this victim is who you are? The victim is an empty shell. Fear is an avoidance of your greatness. Resisting your divinity is futile and painful. It takes much more effort to maintain your smallness than to embrace your magnificence. This is why so many of you are tired a lot of the time. It is really hard work to be unhappy, to resist the natural flow of loving energy offered to you so freely."

"No kidding! I have been feeling too tired to even go for a walk for months."

"Yes, struggle has become a natural way of being in your life. You have been living in a box of your own making. It represents your limited thoughts and beliefs

46

about life. Your greatness lies outside the box where the life you have been avoiding awaits your participation.

"You were born a wondrous being full of love and joy. When you tried to present your gifts to others, they became frightened by them. It reminded them, in a vague way, of the gifts they had repressed when they were rejected as children. So you withheld your gifts because you were made to feel bad. They withheld their gifts for the same reason. Now is the time to reclaim your gifts. Go forth and give of them freely, without attachment or judgment to the outcome. Humanity is waiting for you to come out of your box and lead the way home."

"I thought Jesus came to do that. Why am I being called to do this job? I don't know if I want this kind of responsibility."

"You are not being called to do anything. You made a choice to change the way you live your life. You have been offered the opportunity to do that. If you truly want to be who you are capable of being, you will have access to the same source of energy that creates universes. By the light you are capable of accessing through your soul, you could change everything in your reality. You could save not only humanity but Mother Earth too. This is how great you all are. Every human has the capacity to open to the loving energy that could bring you all home. All you are being asked to do is reconnect to this energy.

"There are a lot of us who have come here to help humanity remember. You are now being offered the gift of a second chance to come home. If you do not wake up soon, Earth will die. This means your physical bodies will die with it. Your souls will have to continue their quest in another form, in another place."

"This will not look good on our resume!" Rob shouted at the world. "I could sure use a coffee break. This is getting to be too much to absorb."

****

"Now this is more like it", Rob said, as he sat down at his favorite stool in his favorite coffee shop.

"Those old farts in the men's cub were beginning to give me a head ache."

The waitress came by and he ordered a double Latte. Cynthia, of course, abstained. 'This is interesting.' he thought. 'I'm not even in my body and I just ordered a latte.'

"This is your alternate reality, Rob. You can do anything you want."

"Would you stop reading my mind. It is quite unnerving." He was only half joking.

"I can't stop. I 'hear' everything you think. This is just the nature of who I am."

"Do these other people see you and can you hear their thoughts too?" he asked, just to make conversation.

"No. These people, like this place, are just figments of your imagination. You are creating this to comfort your mind. If this was your normal reality, they would think you were loony for talking to an imaginary person because they couldn't see me."

"Well, in that case, lets try a different subject." He was beginning to get the hang of this change of venue stuff. He was over his fear of divine retribution so he felt brave enough to ask his next question. "If god is only a fabrication of our imaginations, then who was Jesus? I mean, if god doesn't exist, then he couldn't be the son of god, could he?"

"Well, sort of. We are all children of The All That Is. Jesus was no exception and he clearly stated it. He was a teacher. Actually he has appeared in physical form to a great many peoples, in a great many places, in a great many time frames. His message has always been the same but it has always been misunderstood by your socially conditioned minds.

"There have been a few who have heard his message with their hearts but those who only hear with their ears have manipulated the truth for their own benefit. The religions that were organized around his teachings were created to suit those who sought to gain power over others. They twisted his message of love and brother/sisterhood by including a vengeful god in the formula. They turned fear of its vengeance into an empire to subjugate humanity by withholding the truth.

"After two thousand years, the truths of his teachings are all but lost. Even those who claim to have a personal relationship with Jesus don't believe their own gibberish. This is why so many fall by the wayside. They succumb to the ego's desire to fill the void created by their lack of real connection to their souls. They have no real spiritual understanding and they know it. They get caught in their own lies and eventually go mad from the stress of trying to keep up appearances."

"So, he was a real man, then?"

"Yes. But he was not an ordinary man. He came from a higher plane of existence than most humans. He volunteered to come here because of his great love and concern, to have the lost souls return home. He also materialized as many other great teachers, throughout your history. Most of your religions are based on his teachings from those various lifetimes. But, and this is a big but, you have a chance to make a greater change in the world because you are from the same place as everyone else."

"What is that supposed to mean?" 'Oh no,' he thought. 'Am I ready for this?'

"The Christ entity, in all his manifestations, came here with no social mind and was able to retain the knowledge of who he was and where he came from while he was here. You, on the other hand, are almost entirely a social mind. By breaking the pattern, by taking back control of your thoughts, you can lose this mind and reconnect to your higher consciousness. The Christ entity came to bring light to your darkness but you have an opportunity to break free of the restricting confines of the darkness. You can generate enough light to lead those around you back home"

"That is one hell of a tall order, Cynthia! I'm not sure if I can handle that." Rob was beginning to feel like he was getting in way over his head.

"You are not so special we want you to do something which is beyond the capacity of any other human to accomplish, Rob. Your reaction is just the limitation of your social mind speaking. You are - you all are - being given the chance to overcome your limitations. This is your ticket home, Rob - nothing more, nothing less. You don't have to save humanity or Mother Earth. You are only being asked to wake up to your true Self. Saving the world would just be a side effect of this waking up."

"Holy Shit, Cynthia! You make it sound so damn simple. How can you be so 'matter-of-fact' about such colossally important information? You are laying one hell of a responsibility on me. Every time you tell me some new piece of the puzzle, the immensity of it grows. You know, I only have a finite mind. Give me a break."

"Oh, get a grip, Rob. Take back control of your mind. It's running amuck again," she said with a smile. "Rob. You take yourself and life too seriously. You will never reach a state of enlightenment by being serious. So lighten up!" She still had that peaceful smile on her face. It was beginning to get on his nerves and she knew it. "I'm sorry. I keep forgetting how heavy you guys are. Believe me, I don't want to upset you. It is just that you know enough already to reestablish your relationship with your soul. You know enough to be all you are capable of being. You have all you need and yet you struggle to maintain your stuckness.

"Let it go. Your mind is a steel trap but you are much bigger and more powerful than that. You have seen how easy it can be to get your socially conditioned mind to stop its crippling dialogue. It is time to take control of your thoughts and get on with reestablishing your relationship with your higher Self."

"Yes. You are right, I know. It's just so hard to recognize when my ego takes over control. This is going to take some effort to accomplish."

"Yes but you are already well on your way. Now it is time to return to your physical life to put what you have learned from this visit to work for you. We wish you only happiness in the rest of your experience but it is your choice. Many are given the opportunity being offered you but few are willing to receive it.

"There are no obligations Rob, only choices. You cannot make a mistake. There are no wrong choices. All choices lead to opportunities to forgive and heal. The only possible action that could be construed as a mistake would be the avoidance of learning the lessons that life offers because it always leads to pain.

"Remember, you are responsible for creating your own life experience. Nobody can interfere with it unless you abdicate your responsibility. Be well my friend and know you are loved."

"But..." his voice trailed off.

"Do not fret, dear one. I and the others are always with you."

"Others?"

"Yes. You have several guides who you will be meeting soon. You can call on us any time. Trust your heart. It was designed to serve your highest purpose."

He found himself standing in his apartment. As he watched, the angel figurine in his hand became soft and began to dissolve, molecule by molecule, until his hand was empty. Before she completely disappeared he thought he saw her wink.